What is it?

Jennifer Jacobson
Illustrated by Liisa Richard Bernal

RIGBY

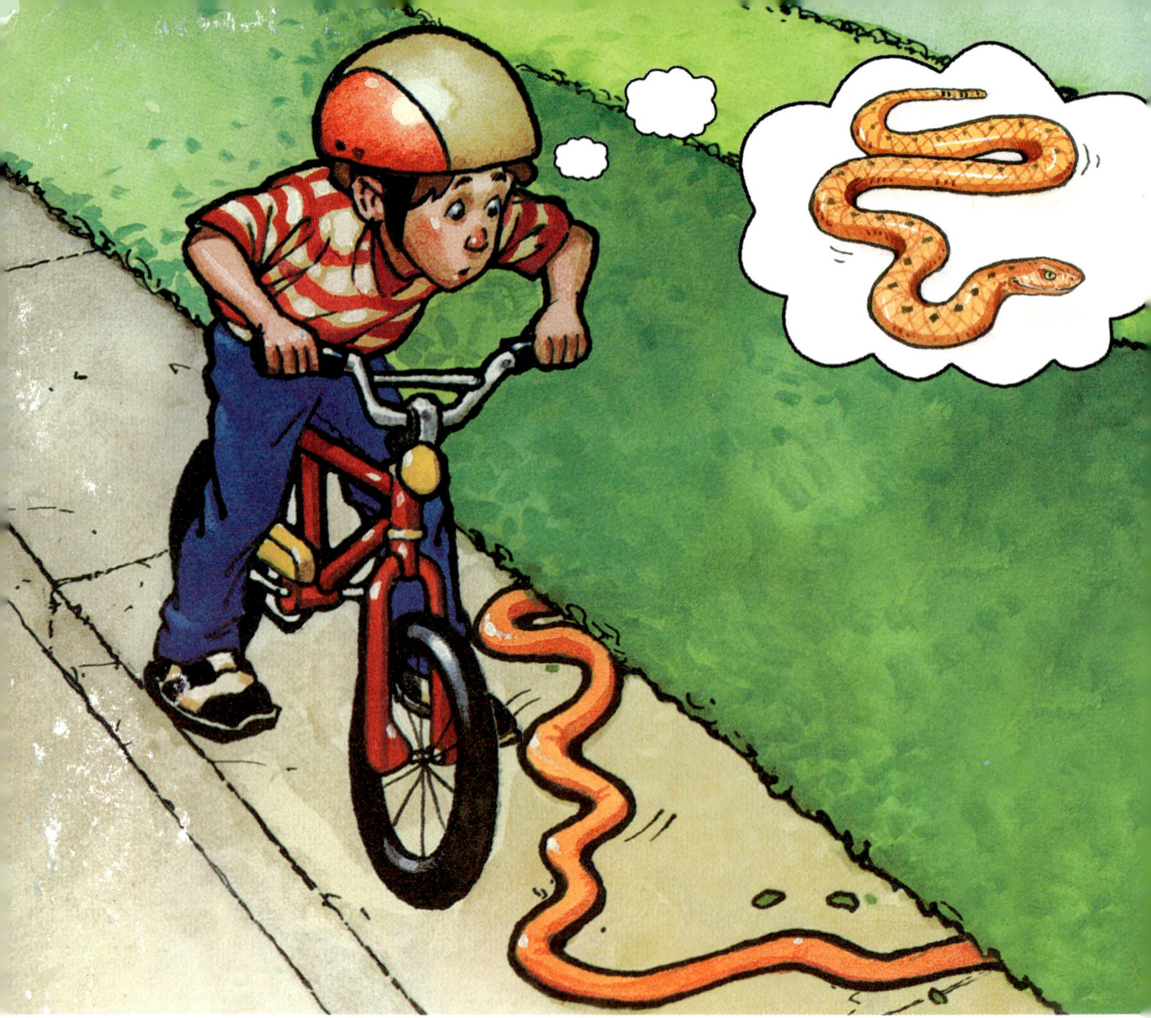

Is it a snake?

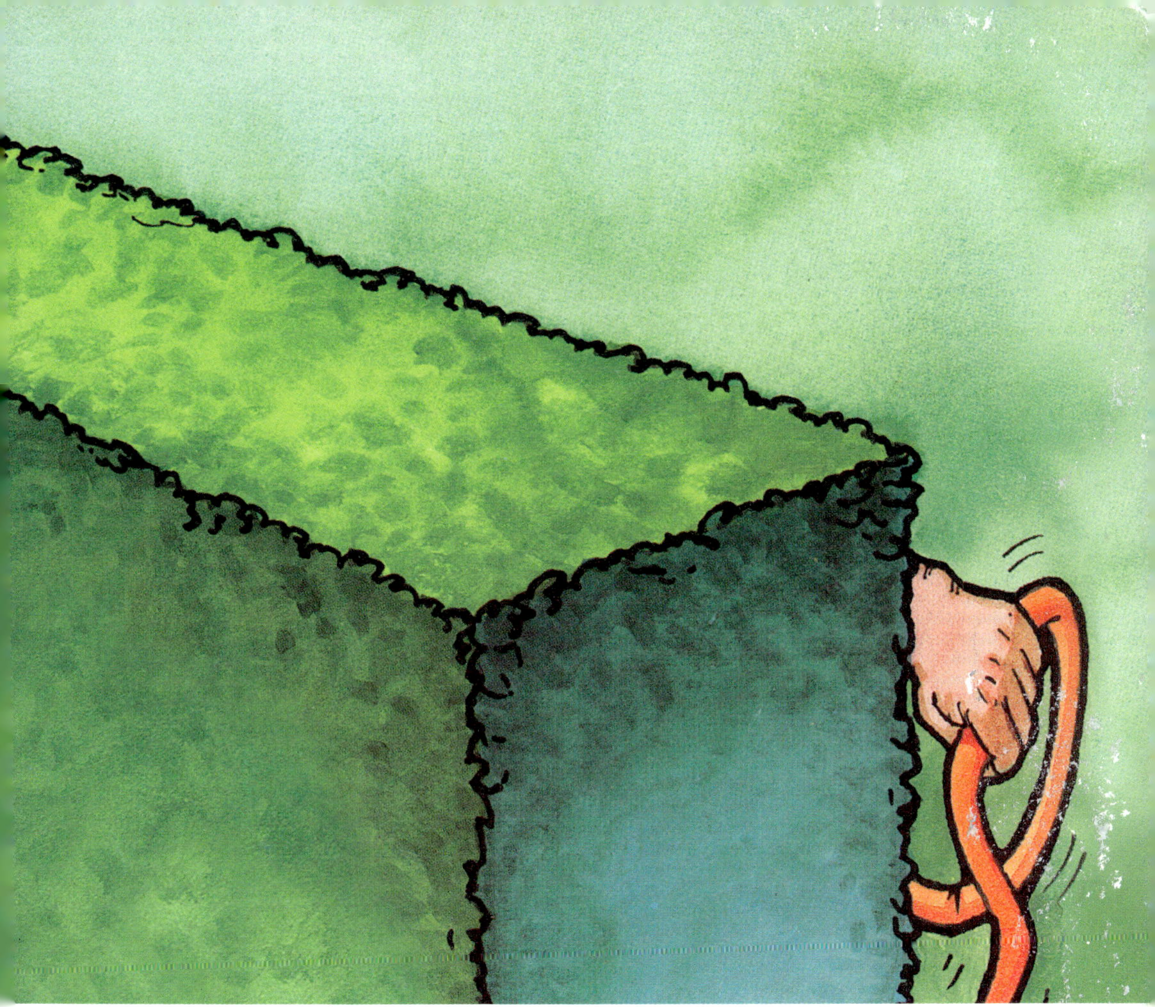

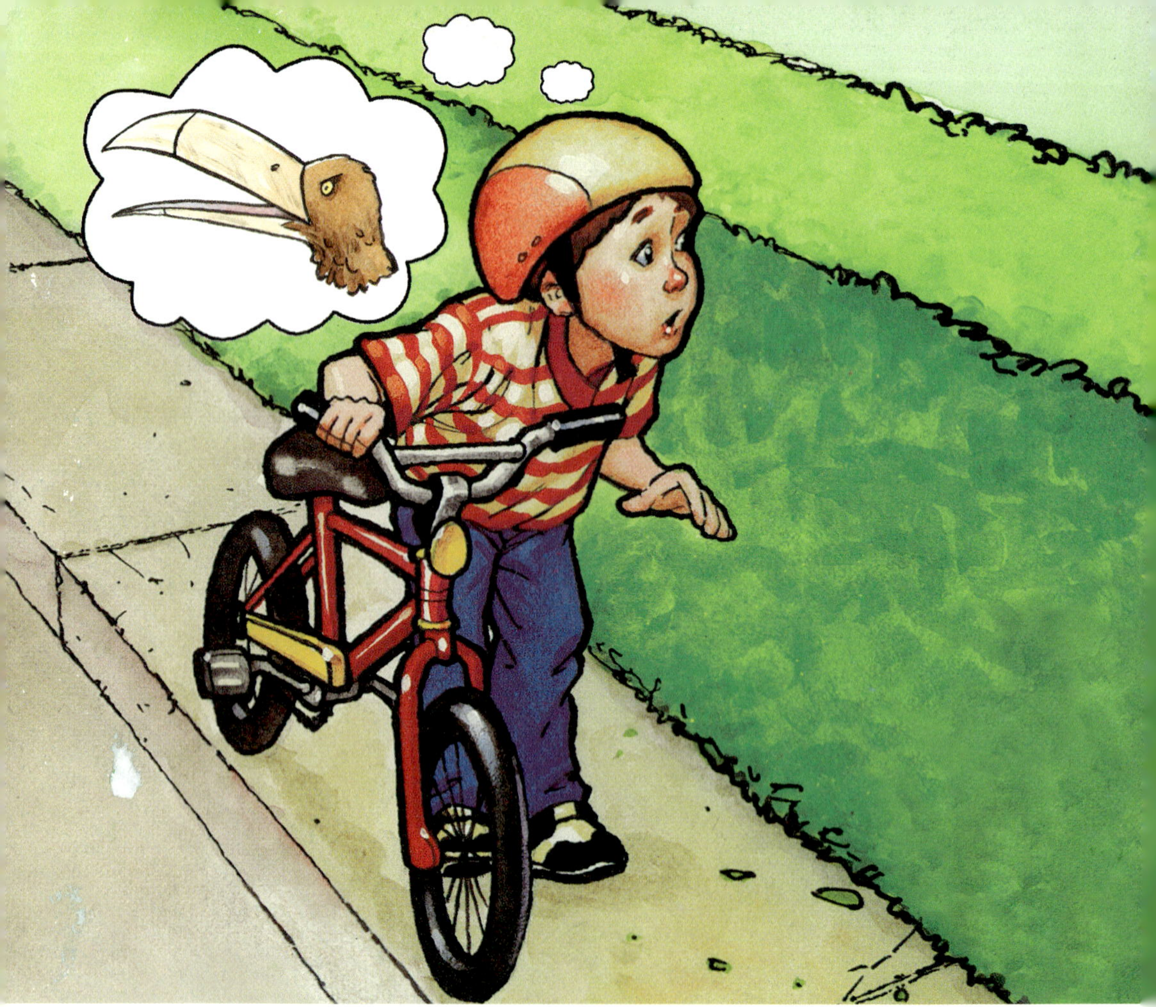

Is it a bird?

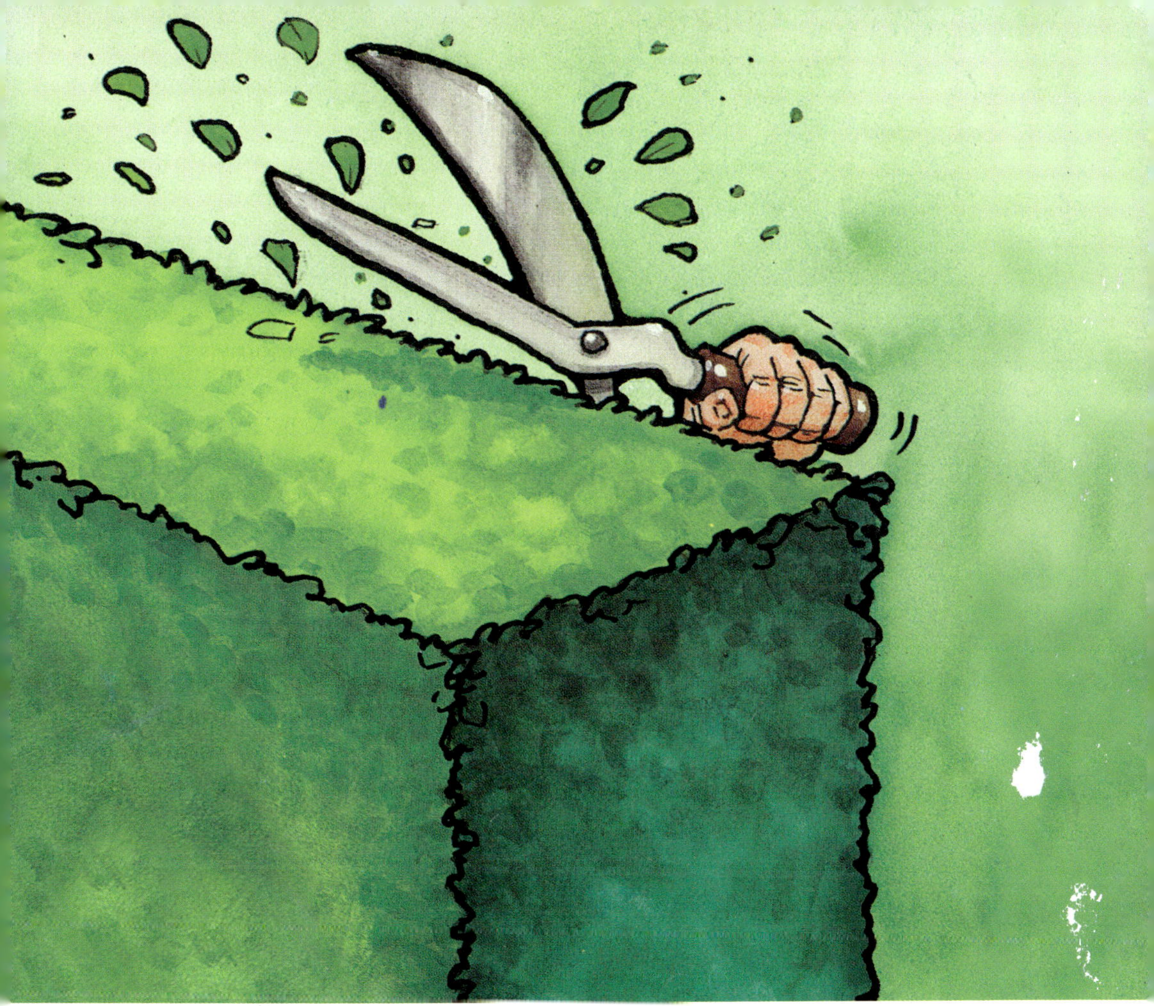

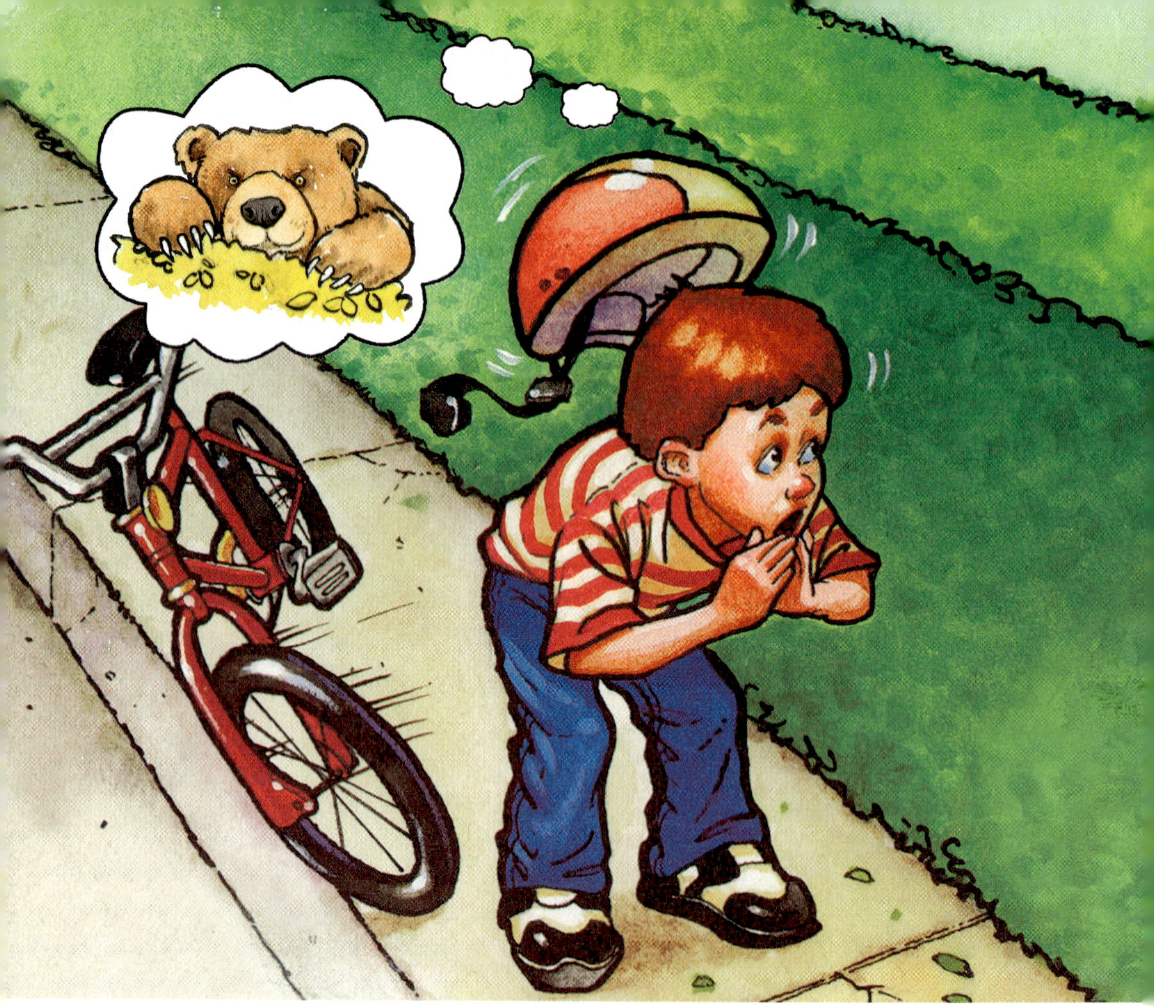

Is it a bear?

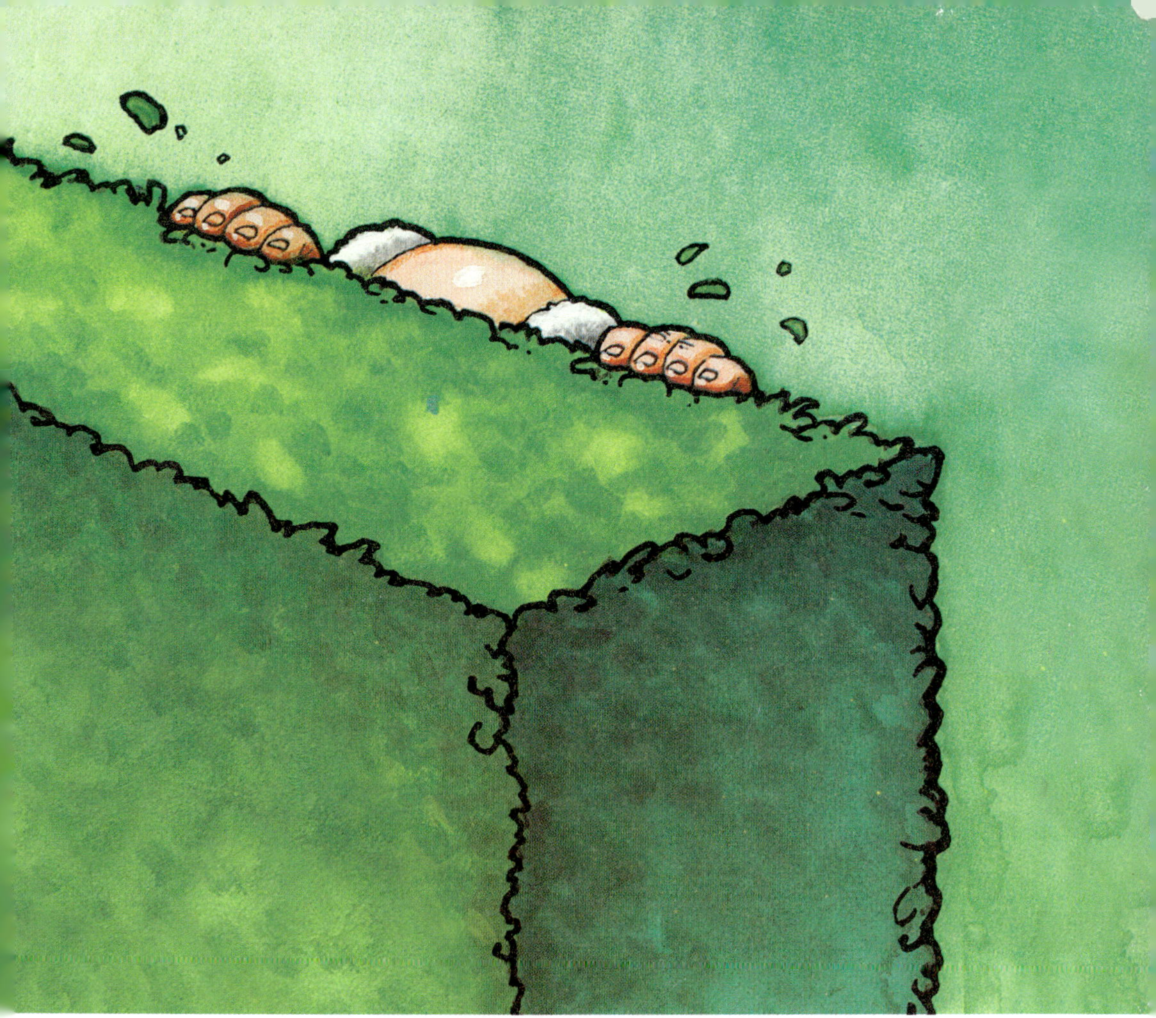

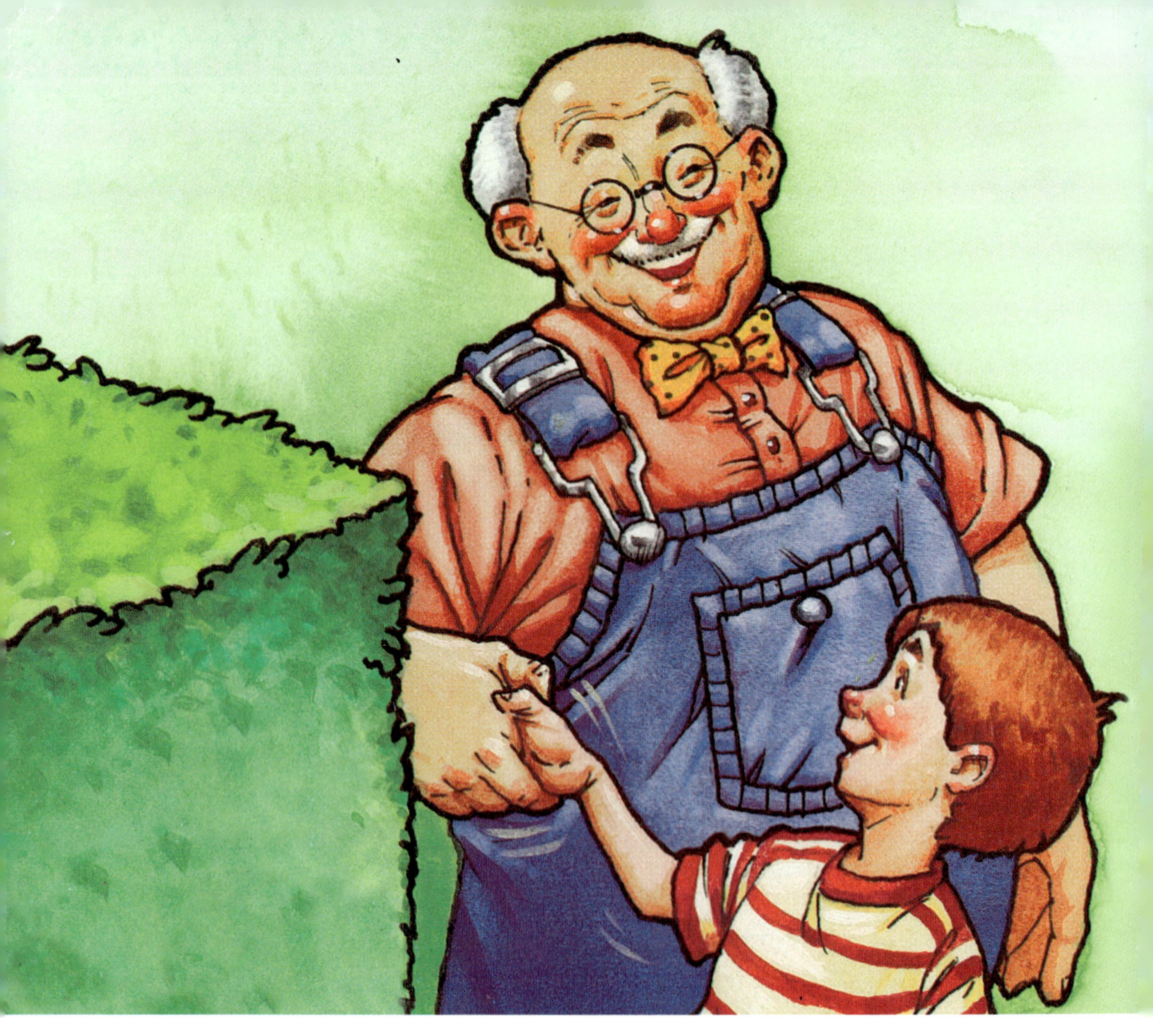

Look! It is Grandad!